WHEREVER YOU

PLUS 7 TOP HITS

WISE PUBLICATIONS
PART OF THE MUSIC SALES GROUP
LONDON / NEW YORK / PARIS / SYDNEY / COPENHAGEN / BERLIN / MADRID / HONG KONG / TOKYO

Dance With Me Tonight

Words & Music by Stephen Robson, Claude Kelly & Olly Murs

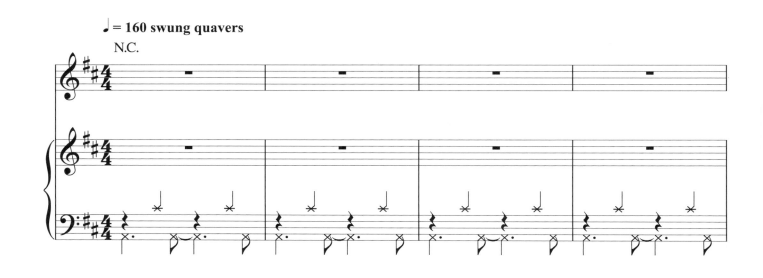

3

you and me could spend a min - ute on the floor up and close get - ting lost in it.

I won't give up with-out___ a fight.___ I just___ wan - na...

Ooh,_____ oh,_____ ba - by___ I just_

___ want you___ to dance___ with me to-night.

To Coda

4

2. We're get-ting sweat- y, hot and heav- y in the crowd now. A - loo- sen up and let your

hands go down, down. Go with it girl, yeah just close your eyes,_

yeah._ I feel the mu- sic go- ing

through your bod - y. A - look- ing at you I can tell you want me.

D.S. al Coda

6

8

Lego House

Words & Music by Ed Sheeran, Christopher Leonard
& Jake Gosling

1. I'm gon-na pick up the piec - es and build a Le-go house.
2. I'm gon-na paint you by num - bers and col - our you in.

If things go wrong we can knock it down.
If things go right we can frame it and put you on a wall.

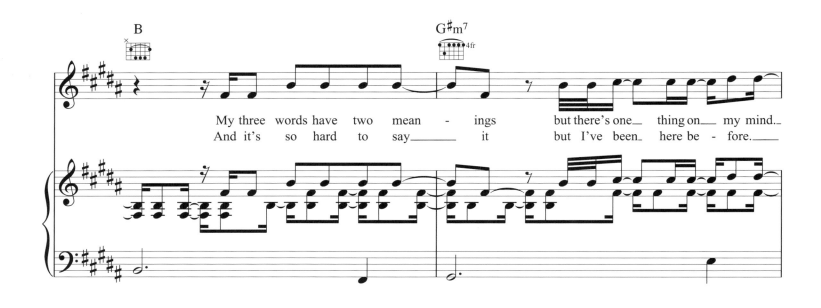

My three words have two mean - ings but there's one__ thing on__ my mind..
And it's so hard to say_____ it but I've been__ here be - fore._____

__ It's all for_____ you, mm._____
__ Now I'll sur -ren - der up my heart_____ and swap it for yours.____

1° only

And it's dark in a cold De-cem - ber, but I've got you to keep me warm..

If you're bro- ken, I will mend ya and keep you shel-tered from the storm that's rag - ing_ on,_____ now.

I'm out of touch, I'm out of love. I'll pick you up when you're get-ting down.

And out of all these things I've done, I think I love you bet- ter now.

I'm out of sight, I'm out of mind. I'll do it all for you in time._

And out of all these things I've done, I think I love you bet-ter now.

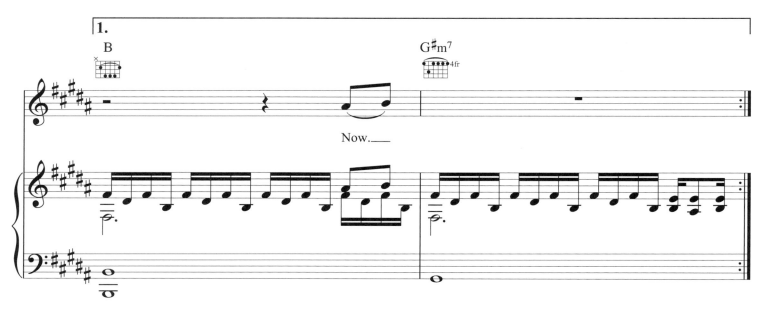

1.

Now._____

2.

Don't hold me down,_____ I think the

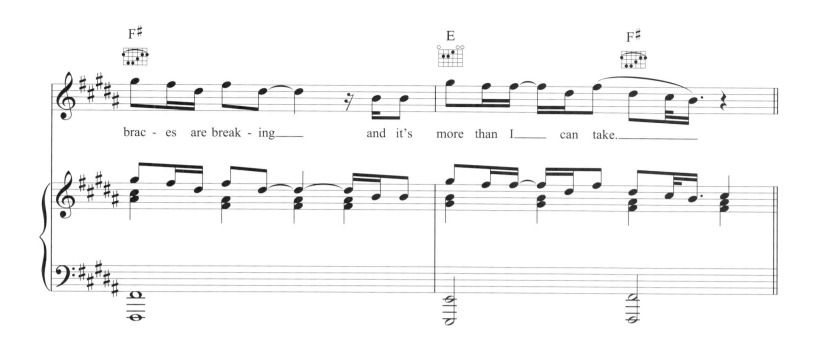

brac - es are break - ing____ and it's more than I____ can take.____

And it's dark in a cold De-cem - ber, but I've got you to keep me warm.__

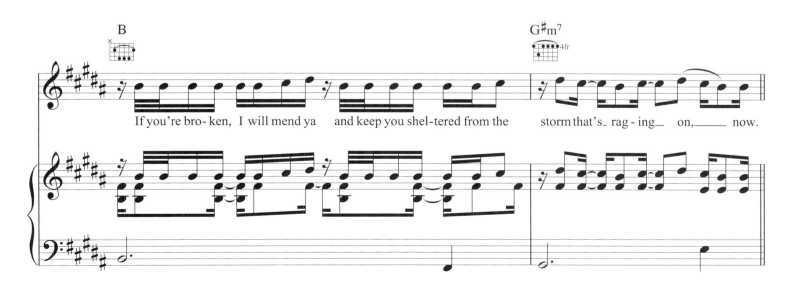

If you're bro-ken, I will mend ya and keep you shel-tered from the storm that's__ rag - ing__ on,____ now.

I'm out of touch, I'm out of love. I'll pick you up when you're get-ting down.

And out of all these things I've done, I think I love you bet-ter now.

I'm out of sight, I'm out of mind. I'll do it all for you in time.__

And out of all these things I've done, I think I love you bet-ter now.

I'm out of touch, I'm out of love. I'll pick you up when you're get-ting down.

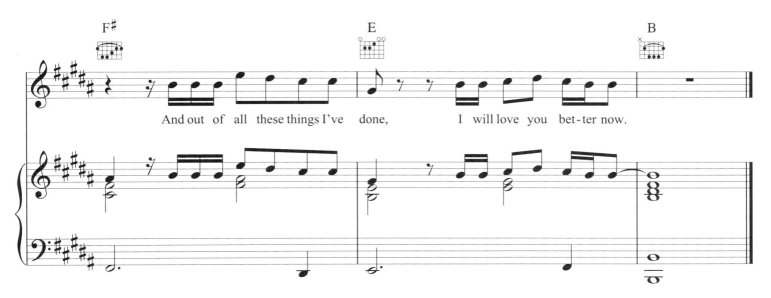

And out of all these things I've done, I will love you bet-ter now.

Marry The Night

Words & Music by Fernando Garibay & Stefani Germanotta

Paradise

Words & Music by Chris Martin, Guy Berryman, Jon Buckland,
Will Champion & Brian Eno

1.

Gm   B♭6   F   C

2.

Gm   B♭   F   C

Ooh,_____   ooh._____

Dm   B♭   F/A   C/E

1. When she was just a girl,_____ she ex-pec-ted the world._____ But it

Dm   B♭   F/A   C/E

flew a-way from her reach._____ So she ran a-way in her sleep_____ and dreamed of

25

2. When she was just a girl,_____ she ex-pec-ted the world._____ But it

flew a-way from her reach,_____ and the bul-lets catch in her teeth._____

Life goes on, it gets__ so heav - y,__ the wheel__ breaks the but - ter - fly.

Ev - 'ry tear, a wa - ter-fall.__ In the night, the storm-y night,__ she'll close her__

pa - ra - pa - ra - pa - ra-dise,   pa - ra - pa - ra - pa - ra-dise,

pa - ra - pa - ra - pa - ra-dise.   Oh,_____ oh._____

La,   la,__ la, la, la,   la,   la,__ la, la, la, la,   la,__ la, la, la,__ la,__ la.__ And so ly-

Video Games

Words & Music by Elizabeth Grant & Justin Parker

1. Swing-ing in the back-yard. Pull up in your fast car,
2. Sing-ing in the old bars. Swing-ing with the old stars.

whis-tl-ing my name.
Liv-ing for the fame.

O-pen up a beer and you say get o-ver here and play a
Kiss-in' in the blue dark. Play-in' pool and wild darts,

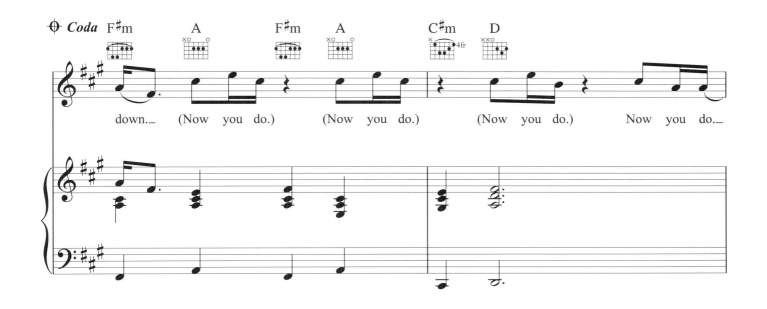

down.__ (Now you do.)   (Now you do.)   (Now you do.)   Now you do.__

__ (Now, now you do.)   (Now you do.)   (Now you do.)__

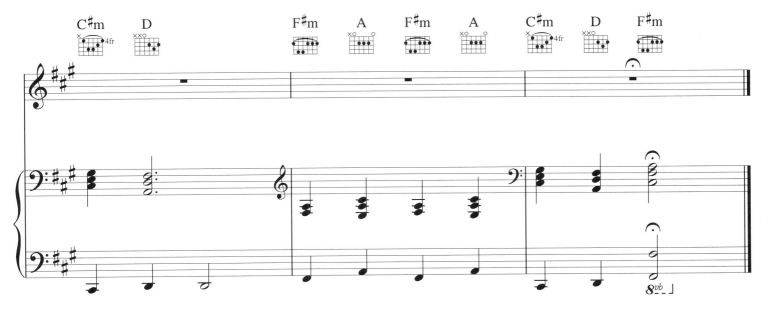

Nothing's Real But Love

Words & Music by Francis White & Rebecca Ferguson

Wherever You Are

Music by Paul Mealor
The text is taken from and/or inspired by poems, letters and prayers provided by some of the
Military Wives, selected and adapted by Paul Mealor, and a passage from St John

heart will build a bridge of light a - cross both time and space._____ Wher -

-ev - er you are,_____ our___ hearts still beat as one,_____ I

hold you in my dreams each night un - til your task is done. Light up the

A

a tempo

dark - ness, my wond-rous star; Our___ hopes and dreams, my heart and yours, for-

rit.　a tempo

-ev - er shin-ing far. Light up the dark - ness, my prince of peace;　May the

rit.

stars shine all a - round you, may your cour - age___ ne - ver

a tempo

cease. Oo._____ Wher - ev - er I am,_____ I will

love you day by day,_____ I will keep you safe, cling on to faith, a - long the dark, dark way._____ Wher -

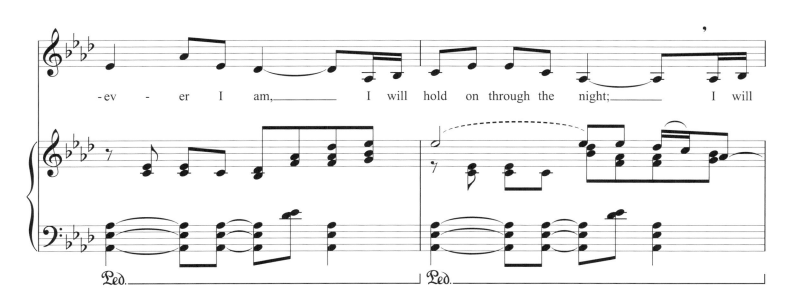

-ev - er I am,_____ I will hold on through the night;_____ I will

peace; May the stars shine all a-round you, may your cour - age____ ne - ver

D rit.

cease. Ah.____

Cou - rage ne - ver____ cease.____

Who You Are

Words & Music by Shelly Peiken, Tobias Gad
& Jessica Cornish

1. I stare at my re-flec-tion in the mir - ror
2. Brush-ing my hair,___ do I look per - fect?

Why am I do-ing this to my - self?_____
I for-got what to do__ to fit__ the mold,__ yeah.__

Los-ing my mind_____ on a ti-ny er - ror.
The more I try_____ the less__ it's work - ing.

I near-ly left the real__ me on the shelf_____ No, no, no, no, no.
'Cause ev-'ry-thing in - side me screams no, no, no, no, no, no, no, no, no._____

Don't lose who you are_____ in the blur of the stars.____

Published by

WISE PUBLICATIONS
14-15 Berners Street, London W1T 3LJ, UK

Exclusive Distributors:

MUSIC SALES LIMITED
Distribution Centre, Newmarket Road,
Bury St Edmunds, Suffolk IP33 3YB, UK

MUSIC SALES PTY LIMITED
20 Resolution Drive,
Caringbah, NSW 2229, Australia

Order No. AM1004828
ISBN 978-1-78038-577-8
This book © Copyright 2012 Wise Publications,
a division of Music Sales Limited.

Edited by Jenni Norey.
Cover designed by Lizzie Barrand.

Printed in the EU

www.musicsales.com

YOUR GUARANTEE OF QUALITY
As publishers, we strive to produce every book
to the highest commercial standards.
The music has been freshly engraved and the book has
been carefully designed to minimise awkward page turns
and to make playing from it a real pleasure.
Particular care has been given to specifying acid-free,
neutral-sized paper made from pulps which have not been
elemental chlorine bleached. This pulp is from farmed
sustainable forests and was produced with special regard
for the environment.
Throughout, the printing and binding have been planned
to ensure a sturdy, attractive publication which should
give years of enjoyment.
If your copy fails to meet our high standards,
please inform us and we will gladly replace it.